BIRTH CONTROL

and

CHRISTIAN DISCIPLESHIP

Second Edition

John F. Kippley

The Couple to Couple League International, Inc.
Cincinnati, Ohio

Publisher
The Couple to Couple League International, Inc.

Location
4290 Delhi Pike
Cincinnati, Ohio 45238

Mailing Address
P. O. Box 111184
Cincinnati, OH 45211
U.S.A.

Telephone
(513) 471-2000

Birth Control and Christian Discipleship
Second edition

ISBN 0-926412-10-8

BIRTH CONTROL and CHRISTIAN DISCIPLESHIP

True or False?_____ No Christian church ever accepted contraception as morally permissible before 1930..

True or False?_____ The anti-contraceptive laws of 19th Century America were passed by Protestants for a largely Protestant America.

True or False?_____ The leaders of the Protestant Reformation were strongly opposed to unnatural forms of birth control.

All three statements are true. If these facts are news to you, this pamphlet will be an eye-opener and may provide you with an enriched perspective on the moral issue of birth control within the Christian Tradition.

I. A BRIEF HISTORY

Contraception is not new. Ancient manuscripts dating back as far as 1900 B.C. record the use of contraceptive materials.[1] Moral concerns about contraceptive behavior are also ancient. The Book of Genesis (38:6-26) carries the story of Onan who was slain by God for a practice that today we call coitus interruptus or withdrawal.[2] A rabbi in the third century of the Christian era noted "the deadly sin of Onan," and in the context the sin is clearly his contraceptive act.[3] St. Jerome in the fourth century complained that his criticism of contraception made him unpopular.[4] Martin Luther never allowed contraception of any sort but instead noted that the purposes of marriage were for husband and wife "to live together, to be fruitful, to beget children, to nourish them, and to bring them up to the glory of God."[5] In his commentary on Genesis 38, Luther called the sin of Onan a form of sodomy.[6] John Calvin noted that Onan had sinned both by defrauding his deceased brother and by his act of coitus interruptus, and he called the sin of Onan a form of homicide.[7]

In short, the moral issue of birth control has risen repeatedly throughout the centuries, but until relatively recently there was no division of Christian teaching against abortion, sterilization and contraception.

This is not to say that Christians have uniformly lived virtuous lives before the modern era. Judging from the growth of birth control organizations during the late 19th century and the early 20th century, it is fair to assume that there was sometimes a gap between the teaching of the Christian churches and the practice of individual couples. It has probably always been this way to a degree with all of the Commandments and especially those dealing with sex.

Protestant Anti-contraception Efforts

For approximately 70 years from the first beginning of the contraceptive movement in the 1860s, the churches resisted. In the United States, Protestant concern was reflected in the passage of a federal law against the manufacture, sale, or possession of contraceptives in the District of Columbia and federal territories; it also forbade the mailing of contraceptives or advertisements for them. Passed on March 3, 1873, and known as the Comstock law after its chief

2

backer, Anthony Comstock, a young Protestant reformer, it was followed by many similar state laws. Catholics in the United States at this time were a small and quiet minority. There is no doubt about it: the anti-contraception laws of the late 19th Century were passed by Protestants for a largely Protestant America. It was also during this same period that the states passed anti-abortion legislation.

The Lambeth Conferences of 1908 and 1920

The Church of England at its Lambeth Conference of Bishops in 1908 discussed and repudiated the practice of contraception. At its 1920 Lambeth Conference the Anglican Church fathers acknowledged the contraception debate but responded, ". . . We urge the paramount importance in married life of deliberate and thoughtful self-control . . ." In Resolution 68 of the 1920 Conference they added, "We utter an emphatic warning against the use of unnatural means for the avoidance of conception . . ."[8]

The Anglican Break: 1930

Thus, it is apparent that in the 19th Century and the early part of the 20th Century, the conviction of Protestant leadership was that unnatural means of birth control were immoral, and this was likewise the constant teaching of the Catholic Church. Despite the fact that reduced birth rates and contraceptive propaganda were making it evident that some or many church members were not living up to the moral teachings, the teaching of the churches had not changed. The beginning of 1930 still saw moral unanimity among Christian churches that unnatural means of birth control were morally wrong, incompatible with a life of Christian discipleship.

"We utter an emphatic warning against the use of unnatural means for the avoidance of conception. . ."
— Anglican bishops, 1920

However, in 1930 a revolution occurred. On August 14 during the Lambeth Conference of 1930, the assembled Anglican bishops broke with the previously unanimous Christian teaching and allowed unnatural birth con-

3

trol devices and practices. Their statement in Resolution 15 is worth repeating since it is historic:

> Where there is a clearly felt moral obligation to limit or avoid parenthood, the method must be decided on Christian principles. The primary and obvious method is complete abstinence from intercourse (as far as may be necessary) in a life of discipleship and self-control lived in the power of the Holy Spirit. Nevertheless in those cases where there is such a clearly felt moral obligation to limit or avoid parenthood, and where there is a morally sound reason for avoiding complete abstinence, the Conference agrees that other methods may be used, provided that this is done in the light of the same Christian principles. The Conference records its strong condemnation of the use of any methods of conception-control from motives of selfishness, luxury, or mere convenience.[9]

The Conference, which passed Resolution 15 with a vote of 193 to 67 (46 not voting), also recognized that up until that time the Anglican Church had taught "that the use of preventive methods is in all cases unlawful for a Christian."[10]

The reaction to this was swift and certain. Pope Pius XI, on December 31, 1930, responded with a teaching letter which contained the following key statement:

> Since, therefore, openly departing from the uninterrupted Christian tradition, some recently have judged it possible solemnly to declare another doctrine regarding this question, the Catholic Church, to whom God has entrusted the defense of the integrity and purity of morals, standing erect in the midst of the moral ruin which surrounds her, in order that she may preserve the chastity of the nuptial union from being defiled by this foul stain, raises her voice in token of her divine ambassadorship and through our mouth proclaims anew: any use whatsoever of matrimony exercised in such a way that the act is deliberately frustrated in its natural power to generate life is an offense against the law of God

and of nature, and those who indulge in such are branded
with the guilt of a grave sin.[11]

If you as a modern reader find that language rather strong, you will find
it quite in keeping with the times when you read some quotations from
American Protestants soon to follow.

"The suggestion that the use of legalized con-
traceptives would be 'careful and restrained' is
preposterous."
— *Washington Post* editorial

The American Sequel: 1931

Within a few months, the Anglican break was echoed in the United
States. On March 21, 1931, the majority of a committee of the Federal
Council of Churches, a forerunner of today's National Council of Churches,
endorsed "the careful and restrained use of contraceptives by married
people," at the same time admitting that "serious evils, such as extra-marital
sex relations, may be increased by general knowledge of contraceptives."[12]

The reaction was immediate and provides a good reflection of that day's
leadership convictions. The first commentary in my possession comes from
an editorial in the *Washington Post* the very next day.

Carried to its logical conclusion, the committee's report,
if carried into effect, would sound the death-knoll of
marriage as a holy institution by establishing degrading
practices which would encourage indiscriminate immorality. The suggestion that the use of legalized contraceptives
would be "careful and restrained" is preposterous.[13]

Strong criticism followed in Protestant church monthlies and from
leading spokesmen:

Birth Control, as popularly understood today and involving
the use of contraceptives, is one of the most repugnant of
modern aberrations, representing a 20th Century renewal
of pagan bankruptcy.
—Dr. Walter A. Maier
Concordia Lutheran Theological Seminary, St. Louis[14]

The whole disgusting movement rests on the assumption of man's sameness with the brutes . . .
—Bishop Warren Chandler
Methodist Episcopal Church South, 13 April 1931[15]

It is of prime significance that the present agitation for birth control occurs at a period which is notorious for looseness in sexual morality. This fact creates suspicion as to the motives for the agitation, and should warn true-minded men and women against the surrender of themselves as tools for unholy purposes.
—Dr. F.H. Knubel, President
United Lutheran Churches
The Lutheran, 2 April 1931[16]

A second line of attack was directed towards the Federal Council of Churches for allowing such a committee endorsement.

Its recent pronouncement on birth control should be enough reason, if there were no other, to withdraw from the support of that body, which declares that it speaks for the Presbyterian and other Protestant churches in ex cathedra pronouncements.
—The Presbyterian, 2 April 1931[17]

Its deliverance on the matter of birth control has no authorization from any churches representing it, and what it has said I regard as most unfortunate, not to use any stronger words. It certainly does not represent the Methodist Church, and I doubt if it represents any other Protestant Church in what it has said on this subject. . .
—Bishop Warren Chandler[18]

According to a booklet written about 1939, "the Northern Baptist Convention at Kansas City and the General Synod of the Reformed Church also denounced the Federal Council for its surrender to human weakness,"[19] and *The Lutheran* of April 2, 1931, noted that "the report of the Federal Council should have been labeled "The Opinions of Twenty-Eight Persons Belonging to Portions of the Christian Church Commonly Called Protestant."[20]

A Brief History   6

Some of the strongest criticism of the Federal Council was in the previously cited *Washington Post* editorial:

It is the misfortune of the churches that they are too often misused by visionaries for the promotion of "reforms" in fields foreign to religion. The departures from Christian teachings are astounding in many cases, leaving the beholder aghast at the willingness of some churches to discard the ancient injunction to teach "Christ and Him crucified." If the churches are to become organizations for political and scientific propaganda, they should be honest and reject the Bible, scoff at Christ as an obsolete and unscientific teacher, and strike out boldly as champions of politics and science as modern substitutes for the old-time religion.[21]

In summary, it is abundantly clear: before 1930, birth control was not a Catholic-Protestant issue. Before August 14, 1930, no Christian Church accepted unnatural forms of birth control as morally permissible. American anti-contraception laws were essentially American Protestant laws.

India

While this booklet is primarily concerned with the Christian Tradition and discipleship, it is worth noting that the condemnation of unnatural birth control was by no means limited to Christians. In the 1920s, Mahatma Gandhi was already fighting the birth control movement, noting that "artificial measures are like putting a premium on vice. . ." Furthermore, "nature is relentless and will have full revenge for any such violations of her laws. Moral results can only be produced by moral restraints."[22]

The so-called sexual revolution started in the Sixties, but that's the 1860s, not the 1960s. . . The real "acting out" of the sexual revolution is best tied to the efforts of Margaret Sanger.

On December 28, 1935, a conference of 2,500 Hindu women condemned unnatural birth control as a sin.[23] When Margaret Sanger visited India in 1936, a thousand people held a protest meeting in Madras. The presiding officer, Mr. S. Satyamurthy, a member of the Imperial Legislative Assembly, reflected the protesters' convictions as follows: "To suggest that you must interfere with the laws of God and try to practice birth control in order to limit the number of your children is, I say, flying against the laws of God; it is almost a blasphemy."[24]

Gandhi clearly believed in the need for some form of conception regulation, but he was totally opposed to contraception.

"There can be no two opinions about the necessity of birth control. But the only method handed down from ages past is self-control or Brahmacharya. It is an infallible sovereign remedy doing good to those who practice it."[25]

The reason Gandhi could speak of the infallibility of Brahmacharya is that it means total abstinence except when consciously desiring a baby. The alternative of periodic self-control during the fertile time was not known to Gandhi in the 1920s. However, in the mid-1930s, probably 1936, during an interview with Margaret Sanger, Gandhi, according to his biographer, "did mention a remedy which could conceivably appeal to him. The method was the avoidance of sexual union during unsafe periods . . ."[26]

From Acceptance to Advocacy

While the Lambeth Conference of 1930 had recommended complete abstinence and had given only grudging acceptance to unnatural forms of birth control, the Lambeth Conference of 1958 more fully embraced the idea of contraception.

"The Conference believes that the responsibility for deciding upon the number and frequency of children has been laid by God upon the consciences of parents everywhere: that this planning, in such ways as are mutually acceptable to husband and wife in Christian conscience, is a right and important factor in Christian family life and should be the result of positive choice before God."[27]

The National Council of Churches on February 23, 1961, gave its backing to unnatural forms of birth control, laying heavy emphasis on motives rather than methods:

> Most of the Protestant churches hold contraception and periodic abstinence to be morally right when the motives are right. . . The general Protestant conviction is that motives, rather than methods, form the primary moral issue provided the methods are limited to the prevention of conception. Protestant Christians are agreed in condemning abortion or any method which destroys human life except when the health or life of the mother is at stake.[28]

. . . a theory that ignored the morality of specific acts except to evaluate them in a grand totality also had to be open to individual acts of adultery and fornication.

A similar line of reasoning was put forth in Catholic circles by the Majority Report of the Papal Birth Control Commission in 1967. Departing from the Tradition, the majority report opted for contraception. They attempted to reconcile this with the teaching of Vatican Council II through a totality hypothesis, according to which contraceptive acts would be redeemed by the overall openness of the marriage to procreation. However, the Minority Report pointed out that such a hypothesis had no way of offering a firm negative to acts of oral and anal copulation or mutual masturbation. It also pointed out that a theory that ignored the morality of specific acts except to evaluate them in a grand totality also had to be open to individual acts of adultery and fornication.[29]

In passing, it may be noted that the totality hypothesis was specifically rejected by the 1968 papal encyclical, *Humanae Vitae*,[30] and Catholic theologians on **both** sides of the issue have acknowledged that "justification" of contraceptive behavior logically entails the "justification" of sexual actions such as mutual masturbation and oral and anal copulation.[31] Do yourself a favor and read that reference at the end of this booklet.

II. THE SOCIAL CONSEQUENCES

Changes in the Civil Law

Just as the 19th Century laws had been passed in the context of the common Christian belief that it was immoral to use contraceptives, so also the law began to change once the unanimity of Christian teaching had been shattered. In 1936, a federal court permitted doctors to import contraceptives on the grounds that Congress had intended to ban only the immoral use of contraceptives and that what physicians did with contraceptives was not immoral.[32] This precedent was followed again in 1939 when a federal court allowed a doctor in Puerto Rico to possess contraceptives. The 1965 Supreme Court case of *Griswold v. Connecticut* sounded the death knell for all anti-contraceptive legislation in the United States. In *Griswold* the Supreme Court invented a doctrine of privacy to shield the marital bedroom from the reach of legislation as far as birth control was concerned and declared anti-contraceptive legislation unconstitutional. Only seven years later, in *Eisenstadt v. Baird,* the Supreme Court extended the same invented right of privacy to unmarried individuals, thus making it clear that its family rationale of 1965 was simply an expedient fabrication.

From Contraception to Abortion

The groundwork for unlimited abortion was laid through the "logic" of the acceptance of contraception. The first step was taken at the 1930 Lambeth Conference which stated that the birth control method "must be decided on Christian principles." As the later widespread acceptance of abortion by people calling themselves Christian was to make clear, that phraseology was open to the widest possible interpretation; so wide, some would say, as to be meaningless. This vague language was used again at the Lambeth Conference of 1958 which spoke of "such ways as are mutually acceptable to husband and wife in Christian conscience." The de-emphasis on any intrinsic meaning of actions in themselves was carried further by the National Council of Churches' 1961 statement as noted earlier: "The general Protestant conviction is that motives, rather than methods, form the primary moral issue . . ."

The final step was taken by the very next sentence in that same NCC statement which is tragic in its irony. "Protestant Christians are agreed in condemning abortion or any method which destroys human life except when

---

. . . that statement, which on the face of it appears to be anti-abortion, is in reality the basis for . . . millions upon millions of abortions that occur each year.

---

the health or life of the mother is at stake." I call this a tragic irony because that statement, which on the face of it appears to be anti-abortion, is in reality the basis for most of the millions upon millions of abortions that occur each year in the Free World. The most common reason given for abortion is typically the "mental health" of the mother, a term broad enough to cover anything from schizophrenia to a headache.

On January 22, 1973, the Supreme Court's doctrine of privacy, invented as a rationale for removing marital sexual activity from the law, was extended to the mother-baby relationship. As long as the baby was not yet born, decreed the Court in *Roe v. Wade,* the mother was free to kill it at any time from conception even up to birth, and all laws prohibiting abortions were declared unconstitutional.

Among Protestant Churches represented by the Church of England and those in the National Council of Churches, it took 31 years to go from the acceptance of contraception in 1930 to accepting abortion for the health of the mother in 1961. In the American legal system, it took 37 years from a 1936 court decision permitting doctors to import contraceptives to the 1973 abortion decision allowing doctors to kill unborn babies. In 1984, a Planned Parenthood abortion facility listed 52 North American churches and church organizations as supporting the right to choose abortion as a method of birth control.[33]

Abortifacient Birth Control

In all probability more newly conceived human beings are destroyed each year by the intrauterine device (IUD) and the Pill than by surgical abortions. An "abortifacient" is a device or drug that causes an abortion. There is no question that both the IUD and the Pill can and do achieve their birth control effectiveness at times by causing very early abortions. In 1989 Mr. Frank Sussman, an attorney for Missouri abortion clinics, argued before the U. S. Supreme Court that "IUDs [and] low dose birth control pills . . . act as abortifacients."[34] The only disagreement comes from certain physicians who want to call themselves pro-life and who also prescribe the Pill, but the reality is that every kind of IUD and Pill has abortifacient properties.

A 1984 pro-Pill pamphlet from the Federal Government notes that
> . . . though rare, it is possible for women using combined pills [synthetic estrogen and progestogen] to ovulate. Then other mechanisms work to prevent pregnancy. Both kinds of pills make the cervical mucus thick and "inhospitable" to sperm, discouraging any entry to the uterus. In addition, they make it difficult for a fertilized egg to implant, by causing changes in fallopian tube contractions and in the uterine lining. These actions explain why the minipill works, as it generally does not suppress ovulation.[35]

From my personal study of pregnancy charts, I am not at all impressed by the ability of thickened cervical mucus to prevent sperm migration into the uterus. This observation has been confirmed by a multi-national study indicating that the days of "sticky" mucus or thick mucus near ovulation are

---

In short, the death toll from the IUD and the Pill may well approach or exceed that of the Nazi Holocaust — each year — in the United States alone.

---

just as fertile as the days of the most fertile type of mucus near ovulation.[36] Resistance to sperm migration does not appear to be a significant factor in the birth control effectiveness of the Pill.

Thus, the only real question is about how often these devices and drugs act as abortifacients, how many early abortions they cause.

The **IUD** is largely off the market in the United States because of massive lawsuits for damages suffered by American women, but it is still widely used in Third World countries whose women do not have access to the courts for similar damages. It has been generally recognized since the early 1970s that the primary action of the IUD is to prevent implantation of the week-old new human life in its embryo stage of development; pro-abortion organizations have used full-page ads to warn that a Human Life Amendment to protect human babies from the moment of conception would outlaw both the IUD and the Pill. In the early Nineties, the question was raised as to whether some types of IUDs did not act more as spermicides than abortifacients, but the question is one of degree: all IUDs have the potential to prevent implantation.

While it is impossible to estimate precisely the number of early abortions caused by the IUD and the Pill, enough is known to illustrate the magnitude of this evil.

In the United States, in 1988 there were still over one million women using the IUD,[37] and they cause perhaps almost three million micro-abortions each year. (See box, "The Arithmetic of Abortifacient Birth Control.")

On a worldwide basis, the figures are simply mind-boggling. A London physician, trying to justify "test tube babies" and frozen embryos, said that if people were really concerned about early human life, "they wouldn't use the IUD which destroys 50 million embryos each month around the world."[38] That would yield the terrifying figure of 600 million early abortions each year on a worldwide basis. I think Dr. Winston was assuming over an 80% pregnancy rate each month, and that's probably high. The 25% rate I have used in the abortifacient arithmetic box yields the still terrifying figure of 247 million early abortions each year based on the estimate of 84 million IUD users throughout the world including 50 million in China.[39]

The Pill may cause more early abortions in the United States than are caused by chemical and surgical abortions. With an estimated 13.8 American women on the Pill, they may well be causing approximately 2,000,000 early abortions each year (see box on abortifacient arithmetic).

In short, the death toll from the IUD and the Pill may well approach or exceed that of the Nazi Holocaust—each year—in the United States alone. What that means is that even apart from surgical abortion, the methods of birth control used by millions of people who call themselves Christian are destroying millions of human lives each year. Add to these figures the early

The Arithmetic of Abortifacient Birth Control

Unobstructed intercourse at the fertile time does not always result in pregnancy. However, the probability of conception occurring for a couple not using anticonception devices (condom, diaphragm, and spermicides) is at least 25% in any given cycle among normally fertile couples of average sexual activity,[40] and it ranges up to 68% for couples who have relations every day during the fertile time.[41] The lower figure (25%) will be used in describing the magnitude of early abortions with the IUD and the Pill; it is conservative relative to the coital patterns stated by Kinsey for American couples where wives are under 40.[42] Thus, a pregnancy rate of .25 in each cycle among one million women using IUDs every cycle would result in 250,000 conceptions per month. An average of 12 menstrual-fertility cycles per year would yield 3,000,000 IUD-caused early abortions. However, since the IUD has about a 5% surprise pregnancy rate, among 1,000,000 IUD users in the U.S.A. there would be approximately 50,000 recognized pregnancies each year, many to be killed later by surgical abortion. Subtracting these 50,000 from the directly IUD caused abortions yields an estimated 2,950,000 early abortions each year caused by the IUD. Multiply that by 84 for the estimate of the world total — 247,800,000 early abortions each year.

Estimates about the number of abortions caused by the Pill are more difficult because of the triple-threat action of the Pill. The older high dosage pills had "breakthrough ovulation" rates of between 2% and 10%;[43] given the lower dosage in today's Pills and the numbers of women using the minipill which apparently has almost no suppression of ovulation, the 10% figure does not seem unreasonable to use, but we can calculate it both ways. Among the 13.8 million American women using the Pill,[44] the 10% rate would yield 1,380,000 ovulatory cycles each month. Applying the 25% overall conception rate would yield 345,000 conceptions each month or 4,140,000 new lives each year, almost all of which would be aborted by the implantation-resisting effects of the Pill.

A 4.7% rate of breakthrough ovulation was observed and reported in 1984.[45] Applying that rate to the 13.8 million American women on the Pill would yield 648,600 ovulations and an estimated 162,150 new lives conceived each cycle, or 1,945,800 each year, almost all of whom would be denied implantation and thus aborted.

Even if you want to use the low 2% breakthrough ovulation rate, a figure I think is too low considering the lower dosages and the minipill today, you will end up with over 800,000 early abortions per year from the Pill alone, about half as many as from surgical abortion. And again, such figures are only for the United States and would need to be multiplied by 4.3 times for the rest of the world.

abortions from IUDs and Pills used worldwide by non-Christians; then add the 50 million surgical/chemical later abortions each year; what you now have are numbers that every year approximate the 250 to 300 million deaths estimated to result from a major nuclear war. It is no small wonder that an increasing number of people are saying that we have richly earned such a holocaust and marvel at God's forbearance in the face of such worldwide contempt for His gift of life.

If the Christian churches had remained firm in their rejection of unnatural methods of birth control, would any of this be taking place? If they had remained firm, I believe there is utterly no question that the present abortion holocaust would only be a small fraction of its present magnitude.

The Sexual Revolution

The so-called sexual revolution started in the Sixties, but that's the 1860s, not the 1960s. In 1798 an economist and Anglican clergyman, Thomas Malthus, started the population scare with the gloomy prediction that population would outstrip the food supply. Malthus recommended late marriage and sexual self-control, i.e., total abstinence, once you reached your desired family size. After Charles Goodyear accidentally discovered the vulcanization of rubber in 1839, the new technology was applied to the manufacture of condoms. Armed with the new condoms, the neo-Malthusians pushed aside the moral beliefs of Malthus and began to promote contraceptive birth control in the 1860s. I call this the beginning of the sexual revolution because it marked the first time in history when people in a "Christian" culture openly and systematically recommended a form of birth control condemned by all the churches as immoral. American Protestantism strongly resisted the neo-Malthusian "philosophy" by passing the previously mentioned Comstock laws in the early 1870s.

Margaret Sanger, best known as the foundress and direction setter of Planned Parenthood, founded her first organization, the National Birth Control League, just before World War I and became the leading proponent of the sexual revolution in the United States. Thus it is fair to say that the real "acting out" of the sexual revolution is best tied to the efforts of Margaret Sanger.[46]

The sexual revolution flourished in the "roaring twenties," but by 1929 national writers were thoroughly condemning it as contrary to human nature.

That revolution might have ended in the 1930s if the Christian churches had maintained the universality of their previous teaching against contraception. Instead, the acceptance of contraception by many of the churches led to a general approval of the attitude that in the modern era it is permissible to take apart what God has rather obviously joined together, the procreative and the affective aspects of sexual relations. With that mentality well engraved in the popular mind, and with married couples publicly welcoming the Pill when it was first marketed in 1960, the flames of the sexual revolution roared out of control in the Sixties and Seventies.

What is called the sexual revolution of the 1960s was the widespread acting out of the basic premise of the sexual revolution, mostly by single men and women, but also by some married couples who got into spouse-swapping and very easy going adultery. The more rebellious might consciously say, "The Bible is out of date. We can take apart what God has put together," but the more common process was to substitute slogans for any sort of thought process. "This is the Sixties! . . . This is the Nineties!" etc., as if the change of a decade was any reason to ignore the moral authority and wisdom of almost 2000 years of Christian teaching. In this acting out process, not only was the God-given connection between sex and procreation denied, but, as predicted, the divinely established connection between sex and marriage has now been weakened to a point unprecedented in Christian history.

Homosexuals also joined their voices to the sexual revolution. No longer did they and others say their orientation was a disease or a weakness. In the Sixties they were linking their behavior to the population scare and were saying that sodomy was not only acceptable behavior but a higher way of life because it did not result in babies.

Humanae Vitae, 1968

Responding to new questions raised by the Pill, Pope Paul VI reaffirmed the Christian Tradition against all unnatural forms of birth control in an encyclical (a teaching letter) titled *Humanae Vitae* ("Of Human Life"), and he was met with tremendous opposition organized by a handful of priests who called for dissent before almost anyone had a chance to read the encyclical.

The Pope was particularly scorned for predicting dire consequences of accepting unnatural forms of birth control. Included in his predictions: a wide and easy road to conjugal infidelity; a general lowering of morality; growing immorality among young people; husbands losing respect for wives and regarding them more as sex objects than as beloved companions; and governments taking coercive birth control action. On the 25th anniversary of that encyclical, July 25, 1993, even its critics were admitting that it was a prophetic teaching.

The Pope, however, did not base his case on the predictable consequences. Rather, he wrote, the teaching "is founded upon the inseparable connection, willed by God and unable to be broken by man on his own initiative, between the two meanings of the conjugal act: the unitive meaning and the procreative meaning" (*H.V.*, n.12).

Personally, I find that terminology difficult because it has so many words of Latin derivation. It seems to me that message might have become more clear if it had been followed by something like this:

> Who put together in one action what we call "making love" and "making babies"? Who else but God? Now, since only married couples have the moral right to engage in sexual intercourse, we call it the marriage act. It is an act which is intended by God to reaffirm the couple's marriage covenant, for better and for worse. We apply to the marriage act the words of Jesus about marriage itself, "What God has joined together, let no one take apart" (Mt 19:6). We have no more right to take apart what God Himself has joined together in the marriage act than we do to take apart what God has joined together in marriage itself.[47]

In summary, the sexual revolution says that you can ignore the God-given connections regarding sex—1) the unitive and procreative dimensions of the marriage act, 2) the permanence of marriage, and 3) the fact that sex is intended by God to be exclusively a marriage act. It is essentially a religious rebellion, for who but an atheist can deny that every unnatural form of birth control is an effort to take apart what God has joined together in the marriage act? If my analysis is correct, the sexual revolution started with the acceptance of marital contraception. Soon, and especially in the United States, it began to affect the institution of marriage itself as more and more couples decided they could break their marriage promises and start new marriages. In the 1960s, the biblical exclusive connection between sex and marriage was widely lost to consciousness, and purely recreational sex gained a certain social acceptance. The "logic" of the sexual revolution went further in the 1980s with increased promotion of homosexual sodomy and the idea that recreational sex of any sort can be had by anyone; mutual consent became the only norm.

The judgment of Luther that unnatural birth control was a form of sodomy was insightful; ironically, the widespread practice of marital contraception has been used to "justify" sodomy.

III. THE MIDDLE WAY:
NATURAL FAMILY PLANNING

There is a special and very tragic irony about the timing of the break with the Christian Tradition against contraception. Between the Lambeth Conference of 1920 which reaffirmed the Tradition and the Lambeth Conference of 1930 which gave grudging acceptance to unnatural forms of birth control, a tremendous scientific breakthrough occurred, one of immense practical significance. In the 1920s and for the first time in recorded history, the time of ovulation was discovered simultaneously and independently by researchers in Germany and Japan. By 1930 this information had been applied to family planning through a system now called "calendar rhythm." To be sure, it had its shortcomings, but its method effectiveness was in the same range as the barrier methods of contraception in the 1930s. Older couples have personally told me that they used calendar rhythm with 100% success all during their fertile years, spacing their children just when they wanted them.

The rudiments of calendar rhythm were apparently known to Pope Pius XI, for in his 1930 encyclical, *Casti Connubii*, he acknowledged the moral permissibility of using periodic abstinence and then having relations in the infertile times.

> Nor are those considered as acting against nature who in the married state use their right in the proper manner, although on account of natural reasons either of time or of certain defects, new life cannot be brought forth.[48]

However, the Anglican bishops in 1930 either were not informed about calendar rhythm or ignored it, and thus they posed a false choice: total abstinence or contraception, two extremes on either side of the middle way of natural family planning with periodic abstinence.

Modern Natural Family Planning

The automobiles of the 1930s have been greatly improved; the same holds true for Natural Family Planning (NFP). The calendar rhythm of the 1930s is referred to today as the Model T of NFP. The Model T Ford served well in its day, but it has been replaced. So also, calendar rhythm has been replaced by methods of fertility awareness that enable a couple to know with great precision when the wife is fertile, even if she has irregular cycles. This is in sharp contrast to calendar rhythm which required regular cycles for its effective use.

Very briefly, modern science has learned that a man is fertile all the time but his wife is fertile only part of the time. Her fertile time extends from several days before she ovulates until a few days afterwards. As her ovaries prepare to release an egg (ovum), she can notice two signs that tell her she has become fertile. Her cervix (the lower end of the uterus or womb) secretes a mucus discharge that assists sperm life and migration. Secondly, the cervix opens up slightly. Women the world over have learned to recognize the mucus sign of fertility; many have also learned how to detect the changes in the cervix although that is an optional part of Natural Family Planning.

After ovulation, her temperature rises, the mucus disappears, and the cervix closes. Thus, a couple can use three signs in a cross-checking way to determine the start of postovulation infertility.

How to make the observations, when to make them, and how to evaluate the various signs of fertility and infertility—these things and much more are taught in NFP classes; this booklet is not the place to go into detail. For those unable to attend classes, the *CCL Home Study Course* has been developed. Call or write the Couple to Couple League for further information.[49]

The type of breastfeeding that normally spaces babies about two years apart has also been rediscovered. In the Couple to Couple League for Natural Family Planning, we call it "ecological breastfeeding," and we distinguish it sharply from "cultural nursing." The latter usually has little effect on the return of fertility after childbirth. With ecological breastfeeding, it is common for a mother to go 12 to 16 months before her first postpartum period. Again, this booklet is not the place to explain the big differences between ecological breastfeeding and the much more common cultural nursing. Further information may be obtained from the CCL user's manual, *The Art of Natural Family*

Planning, and from a brochure, "Breastfeeding: Does It Really Space Babies?"[50]

A personal witness is sometimes helpful. My wife and I have five children. The first was conceived while practicing a hearsay, erroneous version of calendar rhythm. A combination of ecological breastfeeding and the Sympto-Thermal Method spaced out the next births at intervals of 2 years, 2 years, 4 years and 7 years. (No surprises; the last was conceived very deliberately.) It works, and it has been fourteen years since the last birth.

NFP: Not Contraception

The practice of Natural Family Planning must be distinguished from contraception. The "end" or purpose of family planning does not make all the various "means" morally the same. We readily acknowledge this in every area of life. If a couple want to live in a nice house, that end does not make morally the same the various ways of getting there; and, let's face it, immoral means will probably get that house paid for sooner. For example, the couple will most likely make more money and do it faster by illegal drug trafficking than by hard work at an honest business or trade.

By its very nature, contraceptive behavior seeks to take apart what God in His wisdom has put together—the affective and the procreative aspects of

---

Natural Family Planning is, therefore, not a form of contraception; it is the moral opposite.

---

sexual relations. Natural Family Planning, on the other hand, respects God's order of creation; it respects the alternating periods of fertility and infertility that God has established and the integrity of the sexual act as God intends it.

Everyone should be able to see that there is a world of difference between 1) doing something and then trying to evade the consequences of the action and 2) simply not doing anything. It is obvious that couples who engage in contraceptive behavior want to have sexual intercourse at the fertile time of the woman's cycle and yet avoid the divinely ordained natural consequences of such actions, so they take apart what God has put together. On the other hand, the couples who practice NFP with the intention of avoiding or postponing pregnancy simply do not engage in those activities designed by

God to bring about the union of ovum and sperm: they do not have sexual intercourse during the fertile time.

By comparison, consider two individuals who are both tempted to eat excessive amounts of food, but both fear the consequences of being overweight. One overeats and then deliberately vomits; the other simply refrains from overeating.

From biblical times, the first person has been called a glutton, the second temperate. There is utterly no justification for saying they are morally the same simply because both have the intention of not becoming overweight.

Natural Family Planning is, therefore, not a form of contraception; it is the moral opposite. When Natural Family Planning is practiced with the right motives and with prayerful self-control, it can rightly be regarded as one of the fruits of the Spirit (Gal. 5:23).

IV. THE BIBLE AND BIRTH CONTROL

What Does the Bible Say?

"What does the Bible say about birth control?" is a vital question for anyone who accepts the Bible as the word of God. To answer the question very succinctly, first of all, the Bible has a general call to generosity in the service of life, as for example in Genesis 1:28, Psalms 127 and 128. Secondly, the Bible does not address the issue of periodic abstaining from intercourse when there are sufficiently serious reasons for avoiding or postponing pregnancy. However, the Bible not only recognizes the value of periodic abstinence, but in the Jewish cleanliness regulations it actually prescribes 14 days of abstinence beginning with menstruation (Leviticus 15:19,28). I have always thought that was a providential rule for building up the children of Abraham since in typical cycles the couple would be resuming relations at a time of maximum fertility.

Thirdly, the Bible condemns unnatural forms of birth control. It is this latter point that needs further explanation.

An important step towards the restoration of Christian unity concerning love and marital sexuality will be a renewed appreciation of the relevance of the 38th Chapter of Genesis to the subject of birth control. In that account Onan follows an ancient Near Eastern custom known as the Law of the Levirate. According to this custom, if a married man died before he had children, his brother was obliged to marry the widow; their children would be considered as the deceased brother's children.

Onan's brother died, so Onan married the widow Tamar. However, he practiced the contraceptive behavior called withdrawal and deliberately ejaculated outside the vagina. "When he went in to his brother's wife, he spilled his seed on the ground, lest he should give offspring to his brother. But what he did was evil in the sight of the Lord, and He slew him also" (Gen. 38: 9-10).

For centuries the general term among Christians for unnatural forms of birth control was Onanism; indeed, the principle form of unnatural birth control was that of Onan—withdrawal and ejaculation outside the vagina.

23

The Onan account was seen as God's condemnation of unnatural methods of birth control.

However, when belief and practice changed, the Onan account was an embarrassment, to say the least. Thus, a new interpretation was developed which said his guilt was only in his failure to provide a son for Tamar. Which interpretation is correct—the one of centuries or the one that has found recent favor among proponents of contraception?

The first rule of biblical interpretation is that a text must be considered in itself. In the case at hand, the key sentence is, "What he did was evil in

---

When three people are guilty of the same crime but only one of them receives the death penalty from God, common sense requires that we ask if that one did something the others did not do.

---

the sight of the Lord, and He slew him also." Second, the text must be interpreted in the immediate context of the entire account, namely, all of Chapter 38. Third, it must also be seen in the wider context of other biblical condemnations for violations of the Law of the Levirate. Fourth, it must be interpreted in the context of related teaching. Last but not least, it must be seen in the context of the Church's traditional teaching over the centuries lest a person think that the Holy Spirit became operative only today in his guidance of the Church.

1. Biblical scholar Manuel Miguens has pointed out that a close examination of the text shows that God condemned Onan for the specific action he performed, not for his anti-Levirate intentions. The translation "he spilled his seed on the ground" fails to do full justice to the Hebrew expression. The Hebrew verb *shichet* never means to spill or waste. Rather, it means to act perversely. The text also makes it clear that his perverse action was related towards the ground, not against his brother. "... His perversion or corruption consists in his action itself, not precisely in the result and goal of his act. . . In a strict interpretation the text says that what was evil in the sight of the Lord was what Onan actually did (*asher asah*); the emphasis in this sentence of verse 10 does not fall on what he intended to achieve, but on what he **did**."[51]

2. In the context of the entire chapter, Genesis 38, it is clear that Onan is only one of three persons who violated the Levirate. His father, Judah, and his younger brother, Shelah, also violated the Levirate law, and Judah openly

admitted his guilt in verse 26. After Tamar had tricked Judah into having intercourse with her and getting her pregnant, thus getting Tamar accused of harlotry, he admitted, "She is in the right rather than I. This comes of my not giving her to my son Shelah to be his wife."

When three people are guilty of the same crime but only one of them receives the death penalty from God, common sense requires that we ask if that one did something the others did not do. The answer is obvious: only Onan went through the motions of the covenantal act of intercourse but then defrauded its purpose and meaning; only Onan engaged in the contraceptive behavior of withdrawal.

3. The traditional interpretation is reinforced by the wider context of the Bible. The Law of the Levirate and the punishment for violators are spelled out in Deuteronomy 25:5-10. An aggrieved widow could bring the offending brother-in-law before the elders; if he still refused to do his duty, she could "take the sandal off his foot, spit in his face, and say, 'This is what we do to the man who does not restore his brother's house,' and the man shall be surnamed in Israel, House-of-the-Unshod" (Deut 25:9-10). That would be embarrassing, but it is a far cry from the death penalty meted out by God to Onan. It must also be remembered that Deuteronomy has no hesitation about the death penalty for serious sexual sins: chapter 22:22-23 prescribes the death penalty for adultery and for rape. Thus the context of Deuteronomy provides utterly no support for the Levirate-only interpretation of Genesis 38:10. On the contrary, it supports the traditional interpretation that the crime for which Onan received the death penalty was his directly contraceptive behavior.

The anti-contraception interpretation is given further indirect support by the only instance in the New Testament when God metes out an immediate death penalty. In Acts 5:1-11, Ananias and Sapphira went through the motions of a covenantal act but defrauded it, and both were stricken dead after they each engaged in this deception. Onan's responsibility to Tamar was a covenantal obligation; so was the obligation of Ananias and Sapphira to be honest with the apostles. The act of marital intercourse is also a covenantal act intended by the Creator to be a renewal of the faith and caring love pledged at marriage. The Onan account directly supports the Christian Tradition that we are obliged not to defraud this covenantal act by contraception, and the Ananias-Sapphira account shows how seriously God takes the defrauding of covenantal acts.

4. This booklet is hardly the place to relate the anti-contraception teaching of the Onan account to all of the rest of the Bible's teaching on love and sex. However, it can be stated without fear of contradiction that the teaching against unnatural forms of birth control is in perfect harmony with the biblical teaching against immoral forms of sex such as sodomy, fornication, and adultery. It is also in the most perfect harmony with the biblical teaching on love, marriage and discipleship.

On the other hand, as has already been pointed out, the intellectual acceptance of the unnatural sexual behavior of Onan, deliberate ejaculation outside the vagina, has disastrous consequences. Acceptance of one unnatural sexual act as morally permissible provides a sexual logic that cannot say "no" to any imaginable sexual behavior between consenting persons.[52] (Be sure to read this reference.) It is most unpleasant to think about these logical consequences; the number who follow out the sexual logic are still relatively few, but their number is growing. As mentioned previously, at least since the Sixties, practicing homosexuals have called theirs a preferred way of life because their sexual activity is 100% devoid of fertility.

The Religious Force of the Tradition

5. For all practical purposes, the way in which the Church has understood the Scripture throughout the centuries is the most important part of interpretation. It is this which enables us to distinguish between Old Testament affirmations of the natural moral law ("Thou shalt not commit adultery") and mere uncleanness rules, between discipline open to change and truth that is unchangeable. For example, St. Paul spends more words on women's veils in church (1 Cor 11) than he does on sodomy (Romans 1), but the Church has always held that sodomy is a very serious offense against the natural moral law while the matter of veils has been seen only as a matter of discipline.

We have seen that from early Christian times until 1930 there was an unbroken teaching against unnatural forms of birth control. Is this teaching merely old or does it have religious significance? Is it just a matter of discipline or a matter of the natural moral law, the very order of Creation? If you believe in the Last Supper words of Jesus in which He repeatedly promised to send the Holy Spirit to remain with and to lead His Church, then repeated moral teaching has a vital part to play in the formation of your Christian conscience (Jn 14:16,26; 15:26-27; 16:12-14).

Regarding the birth control issue, an Anglican priest wrote in 1965 that it is very difficult for someone who believes that the Church is guided by the Holy Spirit to say that the Church was wrong about unnatural birth control from the first century up until 1930.[53] Yet that is precisely what is at stake. We cannot have it both ways; God does not contradict Himself. If it was true for nineteen centuries that unnatural forms of birth control are against the

---

We cannot have it both ways; God does not contradict Himself. If it was true for nineteen centuries that unnatural forms of birth control are against the very order of creation and are therefore immoral, then how can it be false today?

---

very order of creation and are therefore immoral, then how can it be false today? The issue is not new; God doesn't change; nor does human nature change.

In the 19th Century, American Protestant reformers put their beliefs into action and passed laws against contraception. Since the division of 1930, every pope has reaffirmed the historic teaching in one way or another although, to be precise, this does not include Pope John Paul I, who lived only one month as pope and had no time for a pronouncement. The popes believe that the Christian Tradition against unnatural forms of birth control is the work of the Spirit and that they are obliged to teach it in season and out of season (2 Tim 4:2). They believe that what is at issue is nothing less than the divine truth about human love.

In the New Testament, the Greek "pharmakeia" probably refers to the birth control issue. "Pharmakeia" in general was the mixing of various potions for secret purposes, and it is known that "pharmakeia" were mixed in the first century A.D. to prevent or stop a pregnancy. The typical translation as "sorcery" does not reveal all of the specific practices condemned by the New Testament. In all three of the passages in which it appears, it is in a context condemning sexual immorality; two of the three passages also condemn murder (Galatians 5:19-26; Revelation 9:21, 21:8). Thus it is very possible (indeed, very probable) that there are three New Testament passages condemning the use of the products of "pharmakeia" for birth control purposes. Interestingly enough, there were the same questions about those potions as about the modern pharmaceutical product, the Pill: abortifacient or contraceptive? However, since the Christian Tradition used the term "Onanism" for condemning all forms of unnatural birth control throughout the centuries, our primary emphasis has been on the Onan text rather than on the "pharmakeia" texts.

Many Protestant scholars have commented on the Onan account over the years. They provide ample evidence that pre-Twentieth Century theologians were well aware of the Levirate practice, but they did not teach that the sin for which Onan received the death penalty was solely his violation of his Levirate duty. Charles Provan, an Evangelical Lutheran, did extensive research on this text and published his conclusion: "We have found not one orthodox theologian to defend Birth Control before the 1900s. NOT ONE. On the other hand, we have found that many highly regarded Protestant theologians were enthusiastically opposed to it, all the way back to the very beginning of the Reformation.[54]

In summary, the interpretation that Onan's sin was only the violation of the Levirate custom is a recent accommodation for the practice of unnatural forms of birth control. It is not upheld by the text or the context. On the contrary, the Onan account provides a powerful biblical basis for the traditional Christian teaching that unnatural forms of birth control are immoral. This interpretation is reinforced by certain New Testament passages, and it is certainly confirmed by centuries of usage.

Renewing the Marriage Covenant

There is a further difference between contraceptive or sterilized intercourse and the act of marital intercourse left naturally open to the transmission of life. The Bible condemns every form of sexual behavior except sexual intercourse between a married couple who are not committing the sin of Onan. To put that in a positive way, the Bible teaches us that sexual

---

In short, God intends that marital relations be a renewal of the marriage covenant, a reaffirmation of the faith, love and trust of the couples's own vows when they married.

---

intercourse is a very special act, even a sacred act, that may be used only by two people who have entered into the covenant of marriage, and even in marriage there are some restrictions. While the Bible does not say expressly, "Thou shalt not rape your spouse," marital relations should not be marital rape; such actions would be a gross contradiction of the whole spirit of what St. Paul tells us about marital love in Ephesians 5 and 1 Corinthians 13. The other restriction is that marital relations should not be marred by the sin of Onan.

We are entitled to say that God intends marital relations to be a symbol of the unbreakable marriage covenant that He and the couple have created. In short, God intends that marital relations be a renewal of the marriage covenant, a reaffirmation of the faith, love and trust of the couple's own vows when they married. How do the couple commit themselves to marriage? They promise to love each other with a caring love, for richer and for poorer, in sickness and in health, for better and for worse till their earthly marriage is ended by the natural cause of death. Only after such public vows are they entitled to celebrate their union with sexual intercourse.

Contraceptive (or sterilized) intercourse contradicts this symbolic meaning of the marital embrace. The body language of such acts clearly says, "I take you for better but not for the imagined worse of possible pregnancy and a child." Thus such acts fail to be what God intends them to be—not just a means of relieving sexual tension but at least implicitly reaffirming and renewing the faith, risk, and love of their marriage covenant.

The couple who practice natural family planning respect this meaning of marital relations. Certainly, they may postpone relations despite desire, just as we hope they postponed relations until they were married, despite desire. However, once they engage in the marital embrace, they take it as God created it, placing no impediments and letting it be at least implicitly a renewal of the fullness of their marriage covenant. And, having decided to do nothing to interfere with God's creative work, if God should decide to do some very unusual things—should we say near miraculous?—with very extended life of sperm or ovum, they are more prepared to accept the unasked-for child as a gift from God.

Family Size

The Bible says nothing specific about family size. It does not say we must have as many children as we physically can. However, as we have seen, the Bible certainly encourages generosity in the service of life.

Two questions arise about natural family planning. 1) Can it be used selfishly? Of course NFP can be used selfishly. That's why it needs to be taught within the context of the Judeo-Christian call to generosity in the service of life. However, the fact that NFP can be abused is no reason not to call it a gift from God. Sex is a gift, and it's widely abused; a child is a gift, and some are abused. So let us not criticize a gift simply because it can be abused.

2) If NFP is used selfishly, isn't it the same as using contraception or getting sexually sterilized? No. Selfishness admits of many degrees, from being just a bit less generous than possible to being as stingy as possible. A comparison with another violation of the natural moral law may be helpful. If a rich man directly robs or cheats a poor man, it is very easy to specify the sin. However, if a rich man is not as generous to the poor as he is called to be by God, no one but God can know. When it comes to birth control, it is relatively easy to see that Onanistic acts are specifically against the natural moral law; but no one knows to what level of generosity and family size God is calling a particular married couple. Many couples with two, three, four, and even more children have discovered that the most difficult part of NFP is the decision about seeking another pregnancy.

In the Couple to Couple League, we teach that, in the light of God's call to generosity in the service of life, a couple need a sufficiently serious reason to use NFP. Such reasons may stem from physical or psychological conditions of either spouse or from external conditions such as personal economics and energy, and even social conditions. We encourage periodic evaluation as family circumstances change, and they change every year as the last child becomes a year older.

V. BIRTH CONTROL and CHRISTIAN DISCIPLESHIP

The Future

Will the Protestant Churches which have accepted contraception return to their former position of rejecting all unnatural forms of birth control? It will not be easy or occur overnight; one has only to look at what is happening within the Catholic Church to understand the enormity of the problem. While the popes regularly reaffirm the Tradition against abortion, sterilization and contraception, many priests, educators and laity who have challenged this teaching seem unwilling to admit the fact that they have erred and have often led others astray. This widespread opposition to the official teaching of their own Church will not disappear overnight.

Nevertheless, all things are possible with God. To the best of my knowledge, no Protestant Church has ever issued a statement formally binding that Church to the acceptance of contraception. The Anglicans do not attribute dogmatic weight to their Lambeth resolutions regardless of how well they reflect theological opinion and set directions. The Federal Council of Churches' statement in 1931 was a committee report without binding effect on any of its member churches. Thus no Protestant Church, in returning to

---

. . . the magnitude of present evils makes it evident to any thinking person that good motives alone do not make good moral decisions.

---

its own historic Tradition against contraception, will be faced with the problem of rejecting a pro-contraception doctrine it had been stating to be true as a matter of faith.

Secondly, the magnitude of present evils makes it evident to any thinking person that good motives alone do not make good moral decisions. One convicted Nazi after another claimed that his only motive for killing Jews and Christians was to be obedient to his superiors. Perhaps even Hitler would have

31

claimed a good motive—trying to improve his country's economy. The nuclear debate makes it crystal clear that good motives are not enough: the specific means for promoting peace must be carefully evaluated. It is beyond imagination that the National Council of Churches would say, "The general Protestant conviction is that motives, rather than methods, form the primary moral issue regarding modern warfare." It is to be hoped that all Christian leaders will soon see that the same principles apply not just to international actions but also to interpersonal acts. We absolutely must ask, "What are we considering? What is the nature of the act? What general and specific guidance do we have from God?"

Obstacles to Accepting NFP

In my opinion, the key to unity among Christians about the Christian moral life is a more serious commitment to Christian discipleship. According to the universal teaching of the churches prior to 1930, the use of unnatural methods of family planning was immoral, incompatible with Christian discipleship. Protestant leaders of the day were prepared to call for total abstinence where there was a serious reason to avoid pregnancy rather than to accept the practice of contraceptive behaviors.

Today, the modern Sympto-Thermal Method of Natural Family Planning is highly effective. It is more effective than the barrier methods of contraception; it has approximately the same effectiveness as the Pill and the IUD but has none of their moral and physical problems. The world of the 1920s and 1930s would have been overjoyed to have had the refined natural methods available today. Why, then, doesn't the modern world, especially the Christian world, reject completely the unnatural methods of family planning and embrace Natural Family Planning?

I submit that the answer is a combination of 1) ignorance, 2) lust and 3) fear.

1. Most people are still unaware of the gift God has given us in natural family planning. Such ignorance is the easiest part to overcome. The current availability of NFP instruction is unprecedented. Anyone who can read this booklet can read well enough for self-instruction. We have ample evidence for that from couples who have taught themselves NFP with CCL's *Home Study Course.*

2. Lust is a disordering of the vocation of love, a vocation to which every man and woman is called by reason of being created in the image and likeness of God who is Love (1 Jn 4:16). Lust is not the only disordering of that vocation, but it is the weakness or aberration specifically concerned with the sexual expression of love. The habit of lust can become a very powerful force that leads a person to become sexually aggressive and selfish, to use others as tools for pleasure. In its most hardened form, lust leads to the viewing of pornography and even to using others in pornography and sex slavery as tools for making money. Within marriage, this same disorder can lead a person to reject the idea of sexual self-control. Marital lust can and must be overcome by prayer and penance, like any other moral disorder, and by accepting and practicing self-control.

'Perfect love casts out fear' according to St. John (1 Jn 4:18), and I think the opposite is also true: fear can cast out love.

---

3. "Perfect love casts out fear" according to St. John (1 Jn 4:18), and I think the opposite is also true: fear can cast out love. How often teachers of natural family planning have heard, "I'd like NFP, but I don't think my husband would. I wouldn't even dare ask him!"

What is this which a woman is afraid even to mention to her spouse? Periodic abstinence. Sexual self-control. Not giving in to sexual urges whenever they arise. Being different in a sexually satiated society. Developing the virtue of marital chastity to control sexual aggressiveness and selfishness. Placing sex at the service of authentic marital love.

Sexual self-control inevitably involves some difficulty, and for some it may be the daily cross (for about a week each cycle) that Jesus told us we must carry as the cost of discipleship. However, is not the Christian called to let his love for God overcome his instinctive fear of sacrifice?

There is also a fear of failure that must be overcome. Some people fear that they will fail to understand how to make natural family planning work for them; others fear that the method will fail them. On the first count, it is reassuring to know that the poorest of the poor in Calcutta are practicing natural family planning successfully and that there are teachers of NFP throughout the world who are ready and willing to assist learning couples in every way.

To overcome the fear of the surprise pregnancy, it is helpful to investigate the statistics of all the methods as is done in *The Art of Natural Family Planning*.[55] What you will find is not only that the Sympto-Thermal Method of NFP has a method effectiveness at the 99% level; you also find that NFP has none of the risk statistics of some of the unnatural methods, risks to both health and life.

However, the greatest way to overcome this fear of failure is through increased trust in God, and that is not easy. We live in a technological age in which the vast majority of people in developed countries use chemicals, devices, and surgery to "take care of" their fertility. With Natural Family Planning, a couple learns the mutual fertility God has given them and exercise the divine gift of sexual self-control when avoiding pregnancy. Then, having kept God's laws, they trust that if they should experience a rare surprise pregnancy, His Providence will take care of them.

The Christian Struggle for Chastity

There is a world of difference between knowing that something is wrong and still not doing it; there is a world of difference between knowing that we ought to do something and actually doing it. There is a world of difference between recognizing Jesus the Christ as Lord of the universe and one's personal savior, on the one hand, and following Christ as a disciple. "Not everyone who says, 'Lord, Lord' will be saved, but he who does the will of My Father" (Mt 7:21).

Someone once said, "The trouble with NFP is that it's got to do with sex." What he was saying is that many of us—maybe even most of us—can go from

---

The virtue of chastity is simply essential for the practice of true natural family planning.

---

one year to the next without hardly feeling a strong temptation concerning all the other Commandments, but it sometimes seems we can scarcely go a day without some temptations or pretty severe distractions regarding sex.

Your personal timetable may vary, but I think you know the experience. When it comes to sexual self-control for whatever reason—traveling without your spouse, sickness, natural family planning, lack of privacy, etc.—it is not at all unusual to experience the difference between your current level of virtue or strength and the full discipleship to which you are called. You can and should put away the obvious sources of temptation—sexually provocative magazines, books, movies and television. However, in the last analysis, you cannot get away completely from sexual distractions, fantasies and temptations because you cannot get away from your fallen self.

The power or strength or virtue (the latter word comes from the Latin *virtus,* strength) that enables us to overcome sexual temptations has traditionally been called chastity. It is the spiritual energy that enables us to overcome the selfishness and aggressiveness of the sexual drive and to place sex at the service of authentic Christian love. It goes without saying that we need the help of God to overcome any sort of temptation; the virtues are the good habits that we must develop to cooperate more readily with His grace. The virtue

---

As Jesus taught and as millions of Christians throughout history have experienced, His yoke is sweet, His burden light; and that holds true for the practice of marital chastity with natural family planning.

---

of chastity is simply essential for the practice of true natural family planning. With practice, periodic continence or loving abstinence becomes easier even if never completely easy.

By the same token, the person who develops a habit of giving into sexual temptation finds it easier and easier to sin. The person who fornicates once finds it easier to give in the second time and third time, etc. The person who fornicates before marriage is more likely to commit adultery after marriage. The person who has developed a powerful habit of masturbation will find it very easy to view marital sex primarily as a means of sexual relief rather than as a symbol of sacrificing love. The person who is driven by his or her sexual habits gives up much of the freedom to say "no," and that person may have a difficult time accepting even the idea of the sexual self-control required by authentic natural family planning.

Ministers and priests alike have to deal with their own temptations and are privileged to work with parishioners who are struggling to overcome bad habits of sex and to build the new habits they need for authentic discipleship. Small wonder, then, that a Presbyterian minister wrote me about the difference between our experience of fallen self and discipleship. He reflected upon St. Paul's statement that "we who have the fruits of the Spirit groan inwardly as we wait for adoption as sons, the redemption of our bodies" (Rom. 8:23). The first meaning of that passage may refer to the final resurrection, but it may also bear upon the struggle we experience in walking the narrow way with Christ. The pastor continued: "NFP is a means of redeeming our sexual lives to the glory of God," a bridge between our experience of weakness and our desire for discipleship.

The struggle for the power of sexual self-mastery is clearly recognized by Catholic teaching. In his 1968 encyclical *Humanae Vitae*, which reaf-

---

However, in the last analysis, you cannot get away completely from sexual distractions, fantasies and temptations because you cannot get away from your fallen self.

---

firmed the Tradition, Pope Paul VI stated that this teaching "would not be livable without the help of God, who upholds and strengthens the good will of men" (n. 20). Recognizing the plight of some who feel the chains of habits, the Pope noted, "If sin should still keep its hold over them, let them not be discouraged, but rather let them have recourse with humble perseverance to the mercy of God, which is poured forth in the sacrament of Penance" (n. 25). While the Pope clearly foresaw the immensity of unhappy social consequences resulting from the widespread acceptance of contraception, he still called upon church leaders to treat struggling individuals with great compassion but without ever letting them feel comfortable in their contraception as if it were morally permissible.

In saying, "If sin should still keep its hold over them," I think the Pope foresaw a couple struggling under the habit of past sins occasionally giving into the temptation to masturbate for relief of sexual tension, but I do not think he was including couples who stay on the Pill or IUD, practice sterilized intercourse at the fertile time, or keep foam, condoms, or a diaphragm handy "just in case." Such couples cannot be said to have made a commitment not to sin further in these ways. The real struggle for marital chastity doesn't start until the easy road is renounced and the bridges are burned.

A Christian Perspective

The follower of Christ will not be surprised to learn that natural family planning involves the love of which St. Paul wrote to the disciples at Ephesus: "Husbands, love your wives as Christ loved the Church and gave Himself up for her . . .," a self-sacrificing love that is held up as the model for married love (Eph 5:25).

Yes, natural family planning to avoid pregnancy does require periodic abstinence, but usually no more than is required by the Jewish monthly purification rules (about 12-14 days) and generally less. Natural family planning requires loving and considerate communication between husband and wife. In fact, natural family planning requires spouses to love each other with the love of 1 Corinthians 13, and any couple who have been married for more than a month know the divine and human wisdoms of that recipe for a happy marriage: "Love is patient and kind . . . love does not insist on its own way; it is not irritable or resentful . . . Love . . . endures all things."

As Jesus taught and as millions of Christians throughout history have experienced, His yoke is sweet, His burden light; and that holds true for the

From the perspective of Christian discipleship,
the arguments for contraception quickly wither away.

practice of marital chastity with natural family planning. Better marriages, improved communication, refreshed sex lives, alternating periods of courtship and honeymoon—these are the common reports of those who enter into the practice of NFP with a willing spirit.

In short, every Biblical teaching about the cost and blessings of discipleship, every Biblical teaching about love and sex and marriage applies to the practice of natural family planning when there are sufficiently serious reasons for postponing or avoiding pregnancy.

On the other hand, there can be no doubt about the bitter fruits of contraception. These were recognized well ahead of time by the majority report of the Federal Council of Churches in 1931 as it recognized that "serious evils, such as extra-marital sex relations, may by increased by general knowledge of contraceptives."[56] The year before, Anglican Bishop Charles Gore had warned his fellow bishops that the acceptance of contraception was the opening of a Pandora's box full of sexual and social evils including homosexual practices.[57]

From the perspective of Christian discipleship, the arguments for contraception quickly wither away. The argument that God gave us minds which have developed the condom and the Pill gives no support for the morality of their use. Human minds have also developed the ovens at Auschwitz, early abortion drugs, machinery for cutting small babies into pieces in utero (suction abortion), chemical warfare, child pornography, etc. Discipleship and morality are concerned with what God's people ought to do, not with what is physically possible.

From an economic perspective, there has probably never been a time in the Christian era when the vast majority of Christians have had it so good. If poverty is a problem, the argument is in favor of natural family planning which is cheap and has no risks to health. Furthermore, there has never been a time in all of human history when there was more practical help available to assist couples with natural family planning.[58]

The argument that sexual self-control is difficult is again no argument from the perspective of Christian discipleship, for the Christian knows the message of the daily cross, of the demands of love, of the burden made light, the message of Holy Week and Easter. The Christian disciple also knows of God's loving mercy and forgiveness to those who, like the prodigal son, confess their sins, ask for forgiveness, and resolve to walk the narrow way with their Lord.

Never in the Christian era has the misuse of sex been more widespread or more degrading: one only has to contemplate the phenomena of pornography and the sexual abuse of children; never have the divorce rates been higher; and therefore, never has the truth about the Christian Tradition on love, sex, and marriage been more apparent to those who will search with an open mind and a generous heart. Has not the time come to reverse the moral erosion begun at Lambeth in 1930? Has not the time come for Catholics and Protestants alike to recognize the truth of what their Churches taught in common about married love and sex before 1930? Let us listen again and recognize the prophetic wisdom of the Lambeth statement of 1920:

> We utter an emphatic warning against the use of unnatural
> means for the avoidance of conception, together with the
> grave dangers (physical, moral and religious) thereby
> incurred, and against the evils with which the extension of
> such use threatens the race.[59]

Finally, is not the continuing division regarding the truth about married love a scandal, a stumbling block to non-Christians as well as contrary to the explicit will of our Redeemer?

> That they all may be one; even as Thou, Father, art in Me,
> and I in Thee, that they also may be in Us, so that the world
> may believe that Thou hast sent Me (Jn 17:21).

Christians, let us unite with each other and with our forefathers in a renewed appreciation of marriage, morality, discipleship, and the honest demands of love. We have nothing to lose but the chains of our sins.

REFERENCES

1. John T. Noonan, Jr., *Contraception,* (Cambridge: Harvard University Press, 1965) 9.

2. See "IV. The Bible and Birth Control" later in this booklet.

3. Noonan, 10.

4. Noonan, 101.

5. Noonan, 353n.

6. Charles D. Provan, *The Bible and Birth Control* (Monongahela, PA: Zimmer, 1989) 81.

7. Provan, 67-68.

8. John C. Ford, S.J., and Gerald Kelly, S.J., *Contemporary Moral Theology,* Vol. II, (Westminster: Newman, 1964) 247.

9. Ford and Kelly, 246.

10. Ford and Kelly, 246.

11. Pius XI, *Casti Connubii,* para. 56 (31 December 1930).

12. *New York Times,* 21 March 1931, 13.

13. "Forgetting Religion," editorial in *The Washington Post,* 22 March 1931.

14. J.F.N. (probably J.F. Noll), *A Catechism on Birth Control,* Sixth Edition, (Huntington: OSV Press, about 1939) 31.

15. J.F.N., 31.

16. J.F.N., 30.

17. J.F.N., 30.

18. J.F.N., 31.

19. J.F.N., 31.

20. J.F.N., 30.

21. *The Washington Post,* editorial.

22. J.F.N., 57-58.

23. J.F.N., 58.

24. J.F.N., 58.

25. J.F.N., 57.

26. Mahadev Desai, "Birth Control," *The Ghandi Reader: A Source Book of His Life and Readings* (Bloomington: Indiana University Press, 1956) 306.

27. Resolution 115; cited in Ford and Kelly, 249-250.

28. *New York Times,* 24 February 1961, 16.

29. Leo Pyle, *Pope and Pill* (London: Darton, Longman and Todd, 1968) 257f. The Papal Birth Control Commission was an ad hoc committee set up by the Pope to advise him about the Pill and the various views about birth control. It had absolutely no ecclesiastical authority.

30. Pope Paul VI, *Humanae Vitae*, n. 14, 25 July 1968.

31. For example, M. Valente, who clearly identified himself as a dissenter from *Humanae Vitae,* wrote: "It seems unreasonable to maintain that there is a difference between allowing a husband and wife to use the condom and allowing them to have anal intercourse since neither fulfills the natural law doctrine's requirement of insemination in the vagina. Likewise there is no difference between using the condom and coitus interruptus [withdrawal] or any of the other so-called sins prohibited under the doctrine such as masturbation, homosexuality, and bestiality" [copulation with animals]. To the best of my knowledge, no other dissenter has ever disagreed and tried to prove Valente wrong. Michael F. Valente, *Sex: The Radical View of a Catholic Theologian* (New York: Bruce Publishing Co., 1970) 126. See also reference no. 52.

32. Noonan, 413.

33. "Organizations Supporting the Right to Choose," no listed publisher, literature openly available at the Margaret Sanger Clinic, Cincinnati, on January 19, 1984.

34. *New York Times* (national edition) 27 April 1989, 15. For additional documentation about the abortifacient properties of both the IUD and the Pill, see "The Pill and the IUD" (The Couple to Couple League, 1980) and "The Pill: Is It Safe? How Does It Work?" (CCL, 1993).

35. "Facts About Oral Contraceptives," U.S. Deptartment of Health and Human Services (1984) 3.

36. World Health Organization, "A prospective multicentre trial of the ovulation method of natural family planning. III. Characteristics of the menstrual cycle and of the fertile phase," *Fertility and Sterility,* 40:6 (December 1983) 773-778.

37. William D. Mosher and William F. Pratt, "Contraceptive use in the United States, 1973-1988," *Advance Data,* No. 182 (20 March 1990) 5. Table 4 estimates that 1,158,000 American woman were using the IUD in 1988.

References   42

38. Dr. Robert Winston, quoted by Robert Glass, "Test Tube baby ethics explored," *Free Lance Star* (Fredericksburg, VA) 22 August 1984, 3.

39. Richard Blackburn of *Population Reports,* personal communication, 6 August 1993.

40. C. Tietze, "Differential fedundity and effectiveness of contraception," *Eugenics Review* 50 (1959) 231. Thirty percent of couples discontinuing contraception achieved pregnancy in the very first cycle thereafter. Cited in C. Tietze, "Probability of Pregnancy Resulting From a Single Unprotected Coitus," *Fertility and Sterility* (1960) 485-488.

41. J.C. Barrett and J. Marshall, "The Risk of Conception on Difference Days of the Menstrual cycle," *Population Studies* 23 (1959) 455-461. The authors calculated the probabilities of conception based in coital frequency as follows: once per week = .14; every sixth day = .17; every fifth day = .20; every fourth day = .24; every third day = .31; every second day = .43; and every day = .68.

42. A.C. Kinsey et al., *Sexual Behavior in the Human Female* (Philadelphia: Saunders, 1953) Table 93. For 2,200 white married women, coital frequency per week by age: 21-25 yrs = 3.0; 26-30 yrs = 2.6; 31-35 yrs = 2.3; 36-40 yrs = 2.0.

The coital frequency rate of every fourth day is lower than any of the above Kinsey rates, and Barrett and Marshall calculated a .24 pregnancy probability for such a rate. Therefore the .25 rate used in my calculations is conservative relative to published American coital patterns and the conception probability rates published by Tietze and Barrett-Marshall.

43. John Peel and Malcolm Potts, *Textbook of Contraceptive Practice* (Cambridge: Cambridge University Press, 1969) 99.

44. Robert A. Hatcher and others, *Contraceptive Technology: 1990-1992* (New York: Irvington, 1990) 228.

45. "We are close to lowest steroid dosage in the Pill," *News and Views,* 30 November 1984. Excerpts from the second annual meeting of the Society for the Advancement of Contraception, Jakarta; ed. W. Korteling, (West Orange, NJ: Organon International).

46. See also "The Legacy of Margaret Sanger," (Cincinnati: Couple to Couple League, 1988) pamphlet.

47. The concept that sexual intercourse is intended to be at least implicitly a renewal of the marriage covenant is developed in John F. Kippley's *Sex and the Marriage Covenant: A Basis for Morality* (Cincinnati: Couple to Couple League, 1991). The concept is applied not just to contraception but to each sexual activity condemned by Sacred Scripture.

48. Pius XI, *Casti Connubii* (31 December 1930) para. 59.

49. The Couple to Couple League, P.O. Box 111184, Cincinnati, OH 45211; (513) 471-2000.

50. "Does Breastfeeding Really Space Babies?" (Cincinnati: Couple to Couple League, 1982) 25¢ plus business-sized SASE, or $1.00 postpaid.

51. Manuel Miguens, "Biblical Thoughts on 'Human Sexuality,' " *Human Sexuality in Our Time,* ed. George A. Kelly (Boston: St. Paul Editions, 1979) 112-115.

52. In addition to Valente (see Reference 31), note also the following: "Contraception formally severs orgasm from procreation. This separation not only leaves the sex act sterile, it means that orgasm need not be confined to heterosexual relations and, in fact, not even to a human partner. The justification of contraception must at the same time be the justification of homosexuality and bestiality. For if orgasm can formally be separated from procreation, then, to put matters bluntly, any orifice will do and any instrument that produces orgasm will do. I am not suggesting that people who approve of contraception also approve of homosexuality and bestiality. My argument is that any argument in favor of contraception is in principle an argument for the latter forms of sexual activity. For of two things that are essentially alike, what applies to the one applies to the other. Seal off the penis or vagina so that the sperm cannot fertilize the egg, and it becomes immediately evident that the vagina need not be the only orifice for sexual intercourse, nor the penis the only instrument.

"It is therefore no surprise that, as the practice of contraception becomes increasingly widespread, the incidence of homosexuality should increase massively. The emergence of homosexuality as a socially vigorous phenomenon can be correctly evaluated only within the context of the contraceptive society. Homosexuality is, after all, the ultimate in sterile sexual acts that can be performed between two human beings. It carries to its logical conclusion the self-centered demand for personal gratification which characterizes contraception. Indeed, the disintegration of the family now in progress, involving, as it does, divorce, adultery, child abuse, abortion, premarital promiscuity, and the subversion of the relationship between man and woman to rivalry and bitterness, not to leave out the aforesaid blatant homosexuality, has its source in the contraceptive mentality. For the latter challenges the intelligibility of heterosexuality, marriage and love. Although abortion, sterilization — especially involuntary sterilization — divorce and adultery are more serious issues than contraception, the latter is, in my judgment, the crucial issue underlying all these others. As long as the contraceptive mentality retains its hold on society, it will be difficult, if not impossible, to stem the tide." Raymond Dennehy, "Introduction," *Christian Married Love,* R. Dennehy, ed., (San Francisco: Ignatius Press, 1981) 20-21.

53. R.F. Capon, *Bed and Board: Plain Talk about Marriage* (New York: Simon and Schuster, 1965) 87.

54. Provan, 63; emphasis in the original.

55. John and Sheila Kippley, *The Art of Natural Family Planning* (Cincinnati: Couple to Couple League, 1984) 14-19.

56. *New York Times,* 21 March 1931, 13.

57. Ford and Kelly, 291-292.

58. Universal coverage in the United States will entail regular classes in every rural county and in every major neighborhood in urban areas. In the Couple to Couple League, we are far from that level of service, but we have made progress, more in some areas than others, and we have developed the *CCL Home Study Course* to serve couples in areas where we do not have regular classes. For further information, write and enclose a business size self-addressed stamped envelope to: The Couple to Couple League, P.O. Box 111184, Cincinnati, OH 45211-1184.

59. Resolution 68, The Lambeth Conference of the Church of England, 1920; cited in J.F.N., 30.